Homecoming

Homecoming 3

Summer Solstice 2024

TIME

Aurochs Underground Press

Aurochs3 : Homecoming

ISBN 978-1-7396972-5-9

Published by Aurochs Underground Press, Bath, UK

HOMECOMING

A JOURNAL OF NEW ANIMIST WRITING

Edited by Jack Wolf

List of Artworks

Contents

Ronald Hutton

THE TRADITIONS OF THE SUMMER SOLSTICE

When making any introduction to the associations of a solstice, it may be worthwhile to start by asking what one actually is. This matters greatly, because over the past two centuries the definition and the significance of one has changed in fundamental respects: it is now a moment, when it used to be a process.

Contemporary science makes a solstice the minute when the sun reaches its most northerly or southerly point in relation to the planet, upon the Tropics of Cancer and Capricorn. It can do so because precise modern instruments, and the presence of people in both northern and southern hemispheres who are in communication with each other, makes such an exact timing possible. Thus we can say (for example) that the Winter Solstice of 2023 occurred at a particular minute on a particular day, in this case the morning of 22 December.

In earlier centuries this was of course impossible, and people had a very different experience of what a solstice was. This was based on the fact that the sun appears to travel along the horizon for most of each year, rising and setting at different points, and that is why days and nights get longer or shorter. Around the beginning of June and December, however, its progress seems to slow down, and to the naked human eye it seems to stop moving altogether at sunset on the 20th of each of those months. From then on, it appears to rise and set at the same places on the horizon. Only when it rises on 25 December and 24 or 25 June is it apparent that it has started to move again, and that daylight is now going to increase or diminish again as a result.

That is why the Anglo-Saxons called the darkness that falls on 24 December the Mother Night, or the Night of the Mother(s), and the Romans called the 25th the Rebirth of the Unconquered Sun, or Sun-Return. We of course now generally call it Christmas. That is also why 24 June has traditionally been called Midsummer Day, the equivalent at the other side of the year. It is also why the Romans gave the term solstice to the period when the sun does not appear to move, meaning 'the sun stands still'. It was for traditional peoples a numinous and liminal time, in which the normal laws of nature and of the divine might be suspended. Humans might transcend their accustomed boundaries, to work magic or communicate with superhuman beings. Conversely, spirits of all kinds would be unusually active, and inclined to interact with humans, to the benefit of the latter, or not. It was an exceptionally exciting and dangerous time, and its power rose in the course of it. That was why the most magical night of the summer solstice was the last, that of 23 June, known as Midsummer Eve or Midsummer Night. Christianity matched its dedication of the end of the winter solstice to Christ himself, for his nativity, by giving Midsummer Day to the prophet of Christ, John the Baptist. Its eve therefore became in Christian societies St John's Night or the Eve of St John. Across Europe this was one of the most bewitched and bewitching nights of the year. To the Welsh, for example, it was one of the three 'Ghost Nights', together with May Eve and Halloween.

So what were the particular associations of the summer solstice? It was always neatly paired with that of winter as a balance of matched opposites: light and dark, greenery and barrenness, warmth and cold, freedom and confinement. Two things are at their height at this time: vegetation and daylight. Both naturally featured in its celebration. It is the season when the foliage of trees becomes completely full, heavy and uniform and the grass is at its height and pollinating, while the cereal crops in the fields are fully grown and yet still pure green. Across Europe people traditionally celebrated the midsummer vegetation, especially on Midsummer Eve, by crowning themselves with leaves and flowers, putting up poles woven with foliage and blossoms, and dancing round them, and decorating streets and houses with greenery and blooms. In Britain it was the delicate sprays of birch branches which were taken into churches and houses and hung up in streets. Of flowers, orpen, known as Midsummer Men, and roses, were especially favoured. So were the golden yellow blooms of St John's Wort, not merely for their beauty but their herbal value, as an anti-depressant, and their reputed ability to repel demons. It was said, however, that nobody should pick one after sunset on Midsummer Eve for fear of being plucked up by a fairy horse and then taken at breakneck speed around the district through the dark hours and dumped at dawn far from home. Fairies were indeed thought to be especially active on that night, which is why of course Shakespeare's play about them was given its name. Across Europe to Russia, it was thought that ferns flowered on the Eve of St John, and rapidly generated a miraculous seed which fell from the plant at midnight, and, if gathered, could render the wearer invisible. Naturally witches were thought to revel on this night as the fairies did, a tradition which inspired one of the masterpieces of Russian music, Mussorgsky's 'St John's Night on the Bald Mountain'. It was also one of the great dates for divination, of all kinds, especially to learn the identity of a future husband.

That dense foliage had important implications for the most intimate of human behaviour. In modern tradition it is Maytime, and the Gaelic feast of Beltane, which is most closely associated with love. In most years, however, the temperature around the beginning of May is still too cold for outdoor amorous activity; and the great outdoors were essential to such activity in past times in which households and families were packed together too closely for couples to enjoy any privacy. The early autumn was harvest time, when work was constant and heavy, and exhausting. Early summer, however, was ideal, especially as the weather began to warm up seriously during May, so that by the last week of it, around the Christian feast of Pentecost alias Whitsun, social activities could take place regularly in the open air at last. So could less social, and even more vital, pastimes.

We can tell when the early modern British began to feel sexy from one vital kind of primary source, the parish register, which began to be kept in the 1540s. Among other things it recorded baptisms, which always took place as soon as possible after a child was born. This makes it easy roughly to date conceptions, by counting back nine months from the baptism. The registers reveal that these naturally ran at a low level through the autumn, winter and spring, and shot up in late May to peak at midsummer. This was the time when the evenings were warm, the leaves were dense, the grass was tall and the ditches were dry. Most cities retained a large wood and/or some sheltered lanes with thick hedgerows on their outskirts, which bore often very frank traditional names, for the comfort of their citizens. Midsummer was therefore the festival of what could politely be called love, par excellence.

All this is to miss out the greatest public association of the summer solstice, and the one that matched its qualities of relative warmth and the greatest potential span of sunlight: it was by far the most important fire festival of old Europe. In historic times from the top of Norway to Algeria, and from Ireland to Siberia, Midsummer Eve was the time for kindling flames, consecrating them, and then doing things with them. Those things included making bonfires, and driving livestock round them or between two of them; jumping over those bonfires oneself and dancing round them; carrying torches around the perimeter of cornfields; and processing through city centres bearing tapers, torches and buckets of fire, often accompanied by pageants of the more usual civic kind. These customs were not only universal, but took a long time dying out. Protestants discouraged them as superstitious, but it was really modernity that put paid to them. In England the occasional traditional one has survived, for example at Walton on the Green in Northumberland. Cornwall has staged a wholesale revival since the 1920s, with a chain of bonfires on beacon hills down the length of the peninsula, and a fire carnival now in the streets of Penzance.

So what was all this about? An obvious answer would be sun-worship, when the solar orb was at its height in the sky and length in the day. There is however no actual evidence of this. All the testimony relating to the purpose of the fires, from the Middle Ages onward, focuses on the power of flames to protect, by purifying the air and driving away evil. This is a property that must go back to the Old Stone Age, when our species, leaving Africa, was able with fire to occupy lands too cold in winter for a tropical ape without artificial heating. Cooking with it also much increased the range of available food, and put humans at the top of the food chain. Flaming torches could drive away the most formidable of rival predators, both from meat supplies and from human habitation. If you are camping on an Ice Age steppe, and are faced with something covered in fur, eleven feet long, weighing hundreds of pounds and with teeth like steak knives and you on its menu, pushing a sharp flint on a staff in its face might scare it away. Thrusting a burning brand at it is much more likely to do so. That begs the question, however, of what it was in late summer that made humans so afraid, and inclined to reach for fiery protection. After all, it seems the most comfortable, enjoyable and opulent time of year.

The answer is, a lot of things, which between them made it a peculiarly dangerous season as well as an attractive one. Insects breed at that time more than any other, and whereas now that is merely a nuisance, generating ant or midge bites or fleas on pets, in earlier centuries it was lethal. Fleas carried bubonic plague, lice carried typhus and mosquitoes carried malaria, all serious killers which peaked in late summer and early autumn. Moreover, livestock, out in the summer pastures, and crops, now grown tall in the fields, had become vulnerable to their own epidemics, while storms could flatten whole fields and destroy the harvest. On top of all this, the very factors which made nature so benevolent - the long daylight, warm air, calm seas, low rivers, thick foliage and dry roads – made humans most menacing. It was the peak time for military campaigns, cattle raids, and all manner of crime. No wonder Europeans and their neighbours, for thousands of years, sought magical protection for their selves, homes, fields and animals when it was available at the enchanted time of the solstice, using the great defending element.

We seem therefore to have reached a good-news message in conclusion. In these times when we can pin-point a solstice to the minute, we can ignore its traditional, more extensive and numinous, connotations if we wish. On the other hand, if we choose we can also engage in fire rituals, wear greenery and flowers and deck our homes and social areas with them, try to contact spirits and fairies and engage in divination. We can do so, moreover, without the imminent prospect of being looted, killed, dying of plague or seeing our crops wither or be flattened. That really does sound like the best of both worlds.

Hannah Semple

EARTH'S TIME

I am the sand upon the shore,
Manipulated by means,
Constructed by man
And eternally trapped
In my own being
To meter a rhyme,
But
I am time itself,
Living nature
I am the Earth.
Ever fluid
And forever seeing.

Heidi Smith

THE ORKNEY ISLANDS

Ghosts wander among the mist-shrouded standing stones.
Echoes of the Ancestors wail across time.
Bards chant the bones of Druids, Vikings and Picts.
Hark, the Eagle's deathly lament
As the Raven's banner unfurls.
Warriors flashing swords, the clash of metal,
Wielding justice between clans.
A weaver at her loom braids a tapestry of generations.

Above the islands, the Great Bear guards the land in the dark of night.
The Great Queen watches with wary eyes
As the sun rises on the Son of Christians.

Wind blows cold across the sandy beach and moors of heather
Chilling the skin and bones of descendants
Gathered 'round the stones — to remember.

Sharon Shaw

THE STAG BAR

Althea calls it a bar, but it's really more of a counter; not much other than a large cupboard (one shelf loaded with bread, cheese and fruit, and another containing bottles, mugs and small barrels), a heavy kettle full of hot chocolate standing on a thick plank of time-polished oak balanced in front of it, and a space for her to stand between the two. Behind the cupboard is a short, steep, ladder-like staircase, but the clients don't see that unless they have to climb it. Her bed is up there, but if necessary, there'll be a spare one for those who need a little more shelter than an hour or two at the bar can provide.

There are three stools on the other side of the plank, and behind them a door studded with cast-iron nails. The other side of the door looks different, of course.

Althea never knows their location, not until the clients come in and she can start listening to them, asking them questions, observing their clothes, maybe even catching a glimpse of the outside world when the door opens. The Stag knows, though. He always knows where they are, where they've been, where they're headed. She used to try and ask, but now she's learned to just trust him. It's always the right place; always the right time.

They've arrived, and Althea feels the Stag slowing beneath the bar as he brings himself to a gradual stop. He lowers himself beneath the level of the ground outside, shuffling into invisibility as the bar settles into the environment around it. Althea isn't sure what it'll look like outside, but the brief impression she got from the Stag's thoughts was neon, traffic and rain. A city again, then.

The two of them have been spending more and more time in them lately. Time was, they saw a lot of dark forests; edges of remote villages; sea views from stormy cliffs. That's where the lost folk had seemed to end up before, where they found themselves most in need of a drink, a friendly ear, maybe even a bed for the night. They would linger for a day or two, sometimes longer, while the Stag waited for the next call, and Althea waited for the Stag.

These days they never stay anywhere more than one night.

***

The next morning, Althea mops up the dirt and rain that had blown in through the door when yesterday's clients arrived, and again when they left. Two young men, in love but not aware of it yet, knowing only that they needed to get away from the taller one's friends and the older one's father. Just for an hour or two. Long enough for them to share a quiet drink, a whispered conversation, and enough loaded glances to set the bar on fire, if it had been an especially dry season.

Althea hadn't even needed to say much to them, just a smile when they came in to reassure them they were in a friendly place, a couple of towels to address the rain in their hair, and an occasional observation when they broke their own discussion to ask her for her opinion. She'd noticed that they left holding hands with the confidence of an established couple, which pleased her. Maybe their relationship will last a couple of nights, maybe a few years, maybe a lifetime. It doesn't matter. The connection is the point.

The floor vibrates slightly, and Althea listens for the Stag's message. They will be moving again, and soon. She finishes cleaning the floor and, stowing the mop and bucket under the counter, pushes the drinks cupboard aside to reveal the bedroom stairs. She climbs up, letting the secret door slide closed behind her, and heads up to her bunk. Last night wasn't arduous, but she is still tired. She often is; Althea doesn't remember how old she is, but she knows she's been running the bar for a long time now.

***

This time, when the Stag comes to rest, his thoughts are much quieter than last night. Althea guesses there must be a woodland or a forest nearby. He's taken them to a variety of locations over the years, but he likes to be near trees. She gets a flash of dusk over a cornfield, a handful of distant farmhouses, and... footfalls? Fast ones, getting louder. Someone running towards the bar. They must have arrived just in the nick of time for this one.

The door slams open and a girl, maybe fourteen, maybe a little older but not much, falls inside and drops to her knees. She's panting, half-sobbing. Althea darts out from behind the counter and closes the door quickly; partly because there's always a risk that someone who isn't meant to find the bar will glimpse inside (although not much of one; people are very good at not seeing things that aren't in their immediate field of understanding), but mainly because she knows someone who's trying to flee something when she sees them, and she wants to make sure the girl is safe.

She can't resist a quick glance around the door before she pushes it to, and sure enough she sees trees; a thick wall of trunks topped with a forest green canopy, the last of the daylight disappearing through the leaves. The Stag seems to have squeezed the bar between two trunks, and unless Althea is very much mistaken, the exterior wall is camouflaged perfectly there. The door, when viewed from the outside, looks like a large split in the still-living wood. No one would even spot it unless they were, in sheer desperation, hurling themselves at it in the hope of a place to hide.

Which, of course, is the point.

Althea makes sure they're secure, and then turns to her new client, who is still sitting on the ground, still breathing hard, but now looking around the bar in shock. It is very apparent that she wasn't expecting to find this interior when she dashed into the forest's edge to get away from – whatever had been chasing her. But it's also apparent that she isn't entirely astounded. Her expression is a blend of gradually fading fear, open-mouthed surprise, and something else, especially when she turns and gets a good look at Althea.

Recognition.

"I've seen you before," she gasps.

"You have? When?" Althea doesn't recall the girl, but of course she could have been much younger the first time. If they have met before. Which Althea doubts.

She never gets repeat clients. Never.

"I'm... not sure," the girl says, now looking down at her hands, still on the floor. She's questioning her own memory. Althea knows that feeling when she sees it.

"Would you like something to drink?" she asks. The girl nods, not looking up. "You have hot chocolate, don't you?"

"I do." Althea gets a mug from the cupboard, ladling some of the steaming, rich chocolate out of the kettle. She places it on the counter and the girl gets up, moving slowly to one of the stools and sitting down. She wraps her hands around the cup, staring at it, briefly closing her eyes and breathing in the warm, welcoming scent of the drink.

"Yes, I've definitely been here before," the girl states, after finally taking a drink from the mug and putting it back down on the counter. "You gave me this mug then, too."

"How long ago was that?" Althea asks, cutting herself off before she adds "for you".

"I think I was about four. So maybe ten years?" The girl looks around the bar. "It hasn't changed in here. Like... at all. Although it looks different outside. It was a barn last time."

"It always looks different," Althea replies. "What led you here today?" It is her usual opening question, and she is unsettled enough by the situation that she wanted to try and get the evening back on track.

"Same as last time," the girl says, burying her face in the mug again.

"You didn't want to tell me then, either, did you?" Althea observes, taking a cloth from underneath the counter and wiping some glasses. She's getting some flashes now, of a much younger girl in a muddy, torn shirt and jeans that were already too small for her, stumbling through a field and opening the door of what seemed from the outside to be a rust-coloured barn. They're not her memories, she knows, but the girl's, channelled through the Stag. The girl shakes her head.

"Nora," she mumbles, still staring into the hot chocolate, which is almost all gone. "My name is Nora."

"And what do you need, Nora? You wouldn't have found yourself here unless there was something we could give you. What would help you right now, in this moment?"

"Sleep," Nora replies without hesitation. "I'm cold, and I'm tired. If I could just curl up in the corner for a few minutes..."

"I can do better than that," Althea says, and pushes the cupboard aside. "If you go up those steps, you'll find two bunks. The one with the green quilt is mine, but you're welcome to take the other."

Nora stares at the ladder.

"He won't find me in here, will he?" she asks, her voice shaking.

"He won't find here," Althea assures her. "Folks don't see us unless they need us. That's how it works." Nora nods, and climbs up to the bed. Althea closes the door and goes back to the counter. They will stay here until Nora wakes up.

It frustrates Althea that she still doesn't remember her. She takes out the client diary from the bottom shelf, and opens it from the back. The last few pages are empty, but she comes to the end of the handwritten entries and reads the few scrawled notes about the couple from last night.

London, the location says. There's no date; there never is.

The previous night had been an old man in a high rise flat, missing his wife, wandering the hallways looking for someone to talk to. The Stag had settled them next to the lift, so the fellow found himself face to face with Althea instead of heading down and wandering out into the night; not the safest habit in his part of town.

Before that, a young woman walking the street with a newborn in her arms, trying to find a shop that was still open and might let her have some baby formula, despite the lack of money in her pocket. Not only had the Stag hidden them behind the door of the brightly lit 24 hour garage, but Althea found a box of exactly what the lady needed on the upper shelf of the drinks cupboard. She had made some up for the child, and given them the rest to take home.

Althea keeps turning the pages, back through the weeks and months and years, trying to spot the notes for a four year old girl who had tried to hide in an unfamiliar barn, refused to discuss what was chasing her, and sat quietly drinking hot chocolate until she was ready to leave. She can't find anything.

Eventually she closes the book and puts it back on the shelf. Taking a seat at the counter, on the client side for once, she folds her hands together and stares at her fingers. She picks up the mug Nora had been drinking from and tries to read the cocoa residue at the bottom, as if it were tea leaves.

"No one finds us twice," she thinks firmly, addressing the Stag. She feels his amusement.

Not that you remember, he responds.

"You mean we've had clients come back before? Why isn't that in the book?" She tries not to sound annoyed. Althea doesn't like it when things change; it makes her feel uncomfortable. She's here because... well, she doesn't recall exactly, but she knows the routine of it suits her.

The diary doesn't log second visits, the Stag tells her. Most people get what they need from one. That feeling of safety, of sanctuary... it lasts. They carry it with them. If they need us again, if they have to escape sideways from their life for another evening, something's gone badly wrong. I keep a close eye on them after that. If you look under the counter, you'll find a small address book.

Althea reaches to the back of the shelf under the counter, where she usually finds the cleaning equipment. Eventually her hand closes on a tiny notebook. She flicks through it, and as the Stag suggested, there are only a few entries. Still no dates, and this time no descriptions of why they were here, but as well as locations, this one has names. She sees Nora. Someone called Archie, from Chicago. Elise, who they met in Frankfurt.

And then, at the very beginning... Althea. Cardiff.

"This is me."

Yes.

"I was your first repeat client?"

No. But no one can see anything written before their own entry. And if they come back a third time —

"Yes?"

Well, that means they need complete sanctuary.

Althea stares at the book. At her name. "They stay?"

They do.

"What was I running away from?"

Does it matter, now?

She looks at the book again, closes it, puts it back on the shelf. "No, I suppose not. Will Nora be coming back again?"

She won't need to.

"This isn't her second visit, is it?"

No.

"It's her third."

Yes.

Althea sighs. "When will she take over from me?"

When she's ready.

"And until then?"

She'll sleep.

There is a long pause.

"And what will happen to me?"

The Stag doesn't reply for a good long moment, and when he starts to explain, Althea interrupts him. "I'll sleep."

Yes. Is that all right?

Althea looks at her hands, dry and creased, lined with time, and pain she can't remember, and love, and caring, and support, that she can. She smiles.

"Yes. Yes, I think that would be all right."

Homecoming

Gordon MacLellan

Time?

I am very aware of our human sense of time and how different it is from everyone else's. We are the ones who count and plan and plot the course of the passing years, while there are cousins marking time in hibernation dreams, or the immense cycles of stone or long flights along the charted air that only they know. I think one of the most valuable lessons for animists is to sit beside a tree and sink into their world, however briefly (brief from our side and not even a blink from theirs) Try then to appreciate a different set of perspectives, memories, even identities, grown and regrown, as trees grow and regenerate, divide, clone, reinvent themselves.

BLACK POPLAR

Waiting,
In a discarded corner,
Of a discarded field,
A broken fence,
A threadbare hedge,
No gate, just a spillage,
Of mud onto road,
A handy pull-in.

Waiting here,
Between road and hedge and fence and field,
An enduring patience,

A long cold wait,
On a short, cold day.
Massive,
Muscled,
A giant's torso, reaching up,
With fingers fringing the stumps of arms,
A pollard as forsaken as everything else,
With a last few winter-black leaves,
Fluttering on the last few twigs,
But this bark, rough and welcoming,
Fills my hands,
Root knees offer knuckles,
To rest on,
A journey's pause beside an old friend,
I haven't met before.

No axe is hafted from this wood,
Nor straight-shafted spear,
No coffins, nor sailing ships,
But baskets and boxes
And matchsticks,
Cotton-reels and clogs,
Crucks in barns once,
And beams in houses,
The beds of wagons
And barrels
And the well-smoked walls of hop-kilns.
Once, and once, and once upon a time
Forsaken now,
Forgotten.

Sitting here,
Back to back,
Back to bark,
In the growing dark,
Warmth setting with the sun,
Cold rising,
Cold seeping,
Wood cooling, bone chilling,

Homecoming

Foot and root, arm and branch,
But rough friendly hands hold me
Flesh to wood in this chill twilight,
Losing the edge, my edges,
The separation of skin.

Waiting, watching, patient,
Enduring seasons,
You grew through years of this declining hope,
Did you notice the poplar candles snuffed?
Lights lost, one by one.
I would remember.
I would grieve and brood,
And plot terrible revenges,
But you grew and keep growing,
Spilling pollen into an unforgiving wind,
Standing in this forgotten corner of this forgotten field,
Offering shelter and sanctuary
In an endless optimism.

And how vulnerable am I?
What does it say of me
That a wooden embrace
On a cold afternoon
Can bring me to tears?

VIGIL

We know where the caves are.
We know where the bones lie.
Long bones and skulls, neatly stacked.
And figures come drifting out of the dark of 10,000 nights,
To a small flame on a hilltop.

We know this night.
We know the wind that blows,
Cold over the ridge.
We know the dale and the pass
The Warren Stone holds the river,
The Old Woman watches the track,
The paths were guarded in vain,
And on this cold, winter night
We know the night, the hill, the darkness.
We know this emptiness, this pain.

My words are not your words,
The stories I tell are not the stories you tell.
You told.
But passion crosses the space between our lives,
Our words,
Heartbeats.
Echoes.
My open hand is filled with the hollow of yours,
And I am the only one still with tears to spill.
The touch of stone grounds me,
The breath of wind inspires,
A tree's promise,
A bird's call,
And, voiced and voiceless,
We sing into the long night.

Homecoming

No embrace here, no simple hug, no kiss,
No words to share,
But I'll tell stories anyway,
Over a small flame,
A warmth to call lost souls home.
And here I will sit and share a glass of mead,
With the ancient dead who step out of the shadows.
A love to call lost souls home.

I live in Derbyshire's Peak District and this poem comes out of an annual occasion at the hillfort of Fin Cop. Sitting on that bleak plateau in a cold January evening and offering a point of warmth – fire is tricky here, too many wildfires, too many reckless barbecues, but a token flame works, and offers an invitation that runs across years, breaks our sense of life and time. Those who come, drift in when they chose to…These folk have been here for some 2,500 years (a lot more than 10,000 nights!). Violent deaths, people thrown into the hillfort's ditch, rampart stones pushed onto living bodies. We don't know who they were, these people, why they were killed, but some of them are still here…or maybe they return. After so many years they still come to a flame, a glass of mead and a warm voice telling stories, chanting poems. *Vigil* also references the bone caves that are found now and then in the hills. Different from the Bone Pits where ancient animals fell and died, Bone Caves were possibly ossuaries, depositories for the Dead. Archaeologists and cavers have found some. Others remain hidden.

Search for "Fin Cop, Derbyshire" and "Sculptor's Cave, Hopeman" for more information.

Harriet Sams

UNEXPLODED ORDNANCE AND TOXIC MATERIAL

The Northern Pennines hold a richness of ancient archaeology that abounds with stories, wonders, and mysteries. Not always beneficent, this region has also been a dumping ground for industrial human secrets and land exploitations, ones that people have hoped time and grasses would finally cover over, making them disappear into the shadows of forgotten history.

My journeys onto the moors usually reveal some hidden, and at times painful, truths etched across this semi-barren land, perhaps the remains of lead mines, where barely anything living has colonised the wound. Still raw, after many generations of hiding, exposed on the hillside, they lie, forgotten by humans but embraced by the land.

Today, I walk the dogs up on a road that is new to me. The February wind is sharp, bitter, ready to rain on me. Suddenly I come across a sign, bright red, standing sentinel and alone on the high moor. It reads:

This site contains unexploded ordnance and toxic material. Do not pick up or disturb anything you find as it may explode and cause injury or death.

Shocked into immobility, I become viscerally aware of the lumps and scar tissue in the ground; sheets of concrete, moss-eaten at the edges as it attempted to colonise the surface, ghostly outlines of brick buildings, asphalt roads to nowhere. Up on the horizon is a skeleton of some once-huge structure, now left to collapse and return its abandoned being to the Earth.

What was this place? What on Earth could have happened here? Why is it toxic, dangerous, explosive? Am I safe? Ae my dogs safe, as they try to take bites out of a carcass of a road-killed rabbit? Amongst the enormous site are farms, and sheep. People remain in this place, to farm, to thrive. My mind goes to how they must feel. Is this a landscape they love? Or is it a landscape that keeps others out, a deliberate act of hiding from the outside world? Speculation fizzes through my mind.

I look at the OS map. The entire moor side is marked "storage site (disused)". Truly captivated, I take out my phone and Google it. What comes up stops me in my tracks:

"Experts put residents' mind at rest over moor's dangers

RESIDENTS living near a former RAF base contaminated with chemical weapons have been reassured that the site is safe.

[…….] in County Durham, was used by the RAF during the Second World War as a chemical weapons storage and disposal depot.

After the war the site was cleaned up but an investigation completed in February 2008 showed there were still traces of harmful chemicals such as sulphur mustard, lead and arsenic. Mustard gas causes skin to blister and is also carcinogenic. As a result of the study the Ministry of Defence launched a second, more thorough investigation into the 85- hectare site, which is used for sheep grazing."

I look up from the screen and take in the land around me. Here, on this lonely hill, hidden from the main road by the natural contours of the land, tons of toxic weapons were held, to be shipped eastwards to British and Allied troops to use against other humans. Dangerous work here, for the body and mind. Who worked here? Does anyone still remember this site when it was active? Would anyone tell me? Suddenly I remember my old neighbour Jack, who died last year aged 92. He had been in the Home Guard. Why didn't he tell me of this place? Now I realise he probably knew all along, the site was on his patch, after all. He would have been tasked with protecting it, serving it somehow, no doubt. *Keep it secret, keep it safe.*

For all the shock and surprise which could have let my mind go wild with speculation, the site reaches into me and tells me: stop the frantic wondering. The shriek of a curlew cuts through the racing thoughts, into my mind; Look! Be here, not then, but here now!

Breathing in and allowing for my eyes to focus again outside of myself, the landscape pops back into focus, as if I hadn't really be aware of my surroundings. Sparce grasses sway in the brisk, cold breeze, a kestrel rises high and hovers, gazing down, sheep graze lazily all around. A tinkle and a gush tell of deep-cut water courses. Fallen dry stone walls reach high as far as the land and the eye can go. Alive, yet wounded, this land is. I begin to see how wounds are held, like burning embers of pain, deep inside a soul for all their lives, hidden, shadowy, and if not carefully, lovingly healed, they become the next generations' embers too. What the Earth holds is mirrored within us, and vice versa. What humans have done is still here to be seen, writ large on the landscape. It becomes the living land.

The strong sound of water becomes more insistent. It has rained a lot recently. It has rained a lot since the end of the War. The moor gushes out water that runs past the warning signs and down, into the rivers, into the river Tees and into the oceans. The water cleanses but contaminates at the same time, if that is what it has been given to carry. What are you carrying? *Sorrow.* I shudder with grief, shame, horror at what we have done.

The rain that has been holding begins to fall, sharp onto my face. I have seen enough and decide to turn back. But before I do, I suddenly realise that this place cannot be an orphan from me any more. I know of it now and I want to show it that I see it, I see the underbelly of oppressive wounds and I want to bring these wounds into the light. I go to one of the trackways that must have once led somewhere, a path through looming workshops and warehouses, but now leads only onto cratered moorland. I stop and look around for things with which to make a gift. There is so very little up here, except dead rabbits, gravel and the occasional Pepsi can. I spy two spent shotgun cartridges. How fitting, I think, to make something beautiful with these for such a site. I gather some pebbles and make a tiny cairn, and pull dead reeds from the trackside. I make a bird.

Dissatisfied with what I have made, I fuss, trying to make it more beautiful with what I have. Then I stop, realising that this place has so very little to offer up, but what it has is enough and fitting.

As I walk back to the car, I slow my pace to truly take in what remains above the ground; I cannot help but let strange shapes spin my imagination back in time to the hustle and bustle of the War effort; people in RAF uniform, trucks, shouting, laughter, perhaps. I walk back the final mile, deep in my inner eye, reconstructing this whole world in my mind. What a place to have been and a time to have existed up here. Then I look up and realise that I am surrounded by an emptiness of true orphaning. This wound runs deep, I realise. But for that, the kestrel is still high above, gazing down.

The bird on the ground, in flight, a gift of beauty to this place, flutters in the cold breeze. The dry grasses soften the edges of the bird's body as they sway, and Kestrel overhead shares the wind with this one, encouraging it to fly away with them.

I wonder if a baffled farmer will come across it lying on the crumbling asphalt and wonder at the strangeness of humans.

Just as I leave the site, I spy the bright yellow of ragwort by the outline of a building. Such a dangerous plant. The sheep know instinctively to leave it where it grows, but when it is cut it becomes sweet, and deadly. It nods in the brisk wind and I turn from it, filled with its message: wounded land need to belong too, even burdened with toxicity. No place is an orphan from the circle of life.

Nimue Brown

TIME AND TIDE WAIT FOREVER

Come to the beach, we measure time differently here. Not in the ebb and flow of tides, though, for it is not the pull of the moon that defines time here. This beach is too old for that, and no wave has washed in on this shore for unthinkable amounts of time.

This is a Jurassic beach. I could look up the numbers of years that we count back to identify Jurassic, but it wouldn't help. It is simply too much time. My body refuses to comprehend it, and the numbers slip through my brain like grains of sand on a beach that no longer exists. I cannot count those grains either. Numbers beyond a certain point defy all reason and compression.

The hills of my home are made of limestone. Layer upon layer of history, laid down to form new shapes and places. It seeps into the water passing through it, so I like to think of the limestone as being in me. My bones are the Jurassic sea bed. I am made of ancient life.

There are places where you can visit the Jurassic beach. High on the hills, looking out across the Severn plain, you can also be on a beach that existed first in the unthinkably distant past. Sea shells are common finds, but I have also picked up seaweed, sea urchins and even crabs. It wasn't until I found my first crab shell and had to look it up to make sure my eyes had not deceived me, that I came to understand just how long crabs had been here. The urchins are surprising too, absolutely kindred to their more recent cousins I have found on beaches. An unthinkable amount of time ago, some beings were exactly as we now know them.

Homecoming

They swam here, in a shallow sea that is little more than a dream, now. They lived out the dramas of their lives, to die in this place and sink into stone time, into immortality. Except of course that the shells on the hillsides are not the remains of the long departed. These are memories created by the stone itself, recording the idea of these beings rather than preserving them,

Once erosion brings them to the surface, rain will eat away at them and the stone will start to forget about the Jurassic sea bed. What I have in my bones are the ghosts of the memories my landscape has forgotten.

I am made of time. My more recent ancestors, living on these hills have all been nourished by this water and this soil. We are the ancient dead repurposed. We are the fossil crab become hard water, become bone.

Morgaine Merch Lleuad

TIME DANCE

Cool and smooth, she was sinking, sweetly. She felt the wind soft on her stomach, the hot sun on her eyelids. She smiled. In the trees, the same wind moved the leaves to whispers, woven through and between with the buzzsaw of a drone. She smiled and stretched, slowly, like a cat. The grass beneath was still wet and smelt of earth and rain. All things were well and she smiled. Dropping from the branch onto all fours, she moved to the willow and settled her back against its trunk in piebald half-light. Her garden was warm and wet, cool and shady and alive with words and sounds and greenness. And she was the brown girl, eyes closed and looking for a pale face in the leaves. Waiting. She smiled and sighed, her body purring, tasting the afternoon.

The apples on the tree were filling out, turning gently rosy, although their hidden sharpness would be shocking when they fell into her hand with a quick twist. Sweetness would mean autumn, and languid summer still lingered in her own wild place. She watched the apple tree, reached towards it, and the fruits danced and bobbed in reply. Closing her eyes, she sank back to sleep. After a while, the night passed across the sky, on its way around the world.

And, inside the house, an alarm clock rang for another day.

'Where do I stand to see all of time?'

She rose and moved into the house, where the wheel of the year had spun to point at sharp winter; seasonal turn, sun outside. She lit the fire, breathing frost on the air, and ran to huddle in her furs. Brown skin, brown fur, white fur. One eye watching from the nest, watching flame-flicker and light-curl, watching the fade of two bodies, pale and darker, shadow in the glow. A chrysalis shared her warmth, opening too soon, ancient biology mistaking her own heat for summer's. As she stirred her skins, it flapped with quick little shudders, drying its blues and purples and browns. But when she turned to look more closely, it was gone. Look to the quality of the light through bare branches. Early yet for fragile things to emerge. The rough wool held her, as she slept for a thousand years, waiting for a kiss, or a drop of blood. And time passed, and her brown became faded, and she dreamed in whispers…

…In the city, a mist rose up from the pavements. Among the buildings and the gardens she walked, her long wings shining light with vapour. And all along the ways she moved, until she reached the place where he lay sleeping, upstairs. The huge wings opened, and she rose, holding her fingers lightly to the window, blurred by smoky drops of water. She touched the outline of his sleep and closed her eyes, and waited for him. Time moved, forwards, backwards, spiralling, so that there was all time and none. She warmed her breath to the glass and through, into his dream. And so she saw that he dreamed of a woman with wings outside his window. In his bed, he smiled his wanting and dreamed of her. The winged creature joined the tears from her closed eyes to the mist, and waited for him.

Below, the city stirred and woke, and continued on its grey business. No one had the time to raise their head and see the frozen angel.

'What time is now?'

Time to awake.

Homecoming

The intrusive alarm bell of Spring, jarring sleepers awake. Beginnings, the scent of cold earth and green things under the snow. She felt the itchy vibration of early light in her blood, moving faster, and the skins around her moved against her own, gold skin. She might have slept for hours or seasons, while a blackbird sang in the garden and robins pecked at old bread. A snowman lived there for a while, white, then yellow (a pale face laughing), then melted into the brown and green. And still she waited. No time to wait now. Sliding from her fleeces, spiky cold shocked every hair on her body to trembling. Not for a long moment; hot tea to warm from the inside. Dress in silk and soft wool and leather and create a time. Time for work.

Under the fluorescent lights of the left brain world, time is linear, as it must be, slivered into parts, smaller, bigger. And each fragment joins to the next like plastic beads in a child's necklace, growing, But there is no evolution here. The growth is constant. Predictable. Measurable by the constructs of the measures. Inorganic. Change time: make it fluid, weave it, stretch it and squash it into an acorn as children do. A cobweb spun from time.

In the centre of her garden, she span a thread of bronze autumn and caught it on a branch. Warm fruit and cool, birthing colours of dying leaves. The thread of bread-warm sunlight and frosted ears. Her body fluttered as she danced her weaving around and through the trees to the killing time. Cold, jagged silver, fine and sharp. Blood on the snow from her fingers. Pale face, warm mouth. Weave a hair from your head into this time, binding, as she could not bind him. And then the unbearable green of the new, too bright to cold-dulled eyes, pinpricks of life. Spinning around as the light gets longer, until, breathless and tangled, she falls to lie in lazy heat, the final thread.

And the web is woven. At the centre she sits, like a dewdrop, ready.

'If time is no time, what is 'waiting'?'

A recipe for a day.

Take a measure of early light. Add either an alarm clock or a lover's kiss, depending on preference. Mix together until eyes are fully open. Add clothing to taste, either of your own choosing or as circumstances dictate. Ablute and breakfast as required. Stir until blended. Travel or don't, but remember to stop and smile if tense. Find somethings to do, or watch a cat to see how to do nothing. When your body (or somebody else's) tells you, add food. Listen a lot. Taste everything at repeated intervals. Close your eyes and touch things, unless others are on a low-tolerance diet. Leave to marinate until ready. Add cream, add the smell of apples, add fear and loathing to taste. Stir once more, carefully, deliberately or frantically. When you have finished doing something or nothing, find yourself in your own place. Serve hot, cold or throw away. Ignore, cherish or scream your day.

'Is time outside of us? Or inside?'

She is marking her time by the loudness of a raindrop, by the length of the grass growing up between her breasts as she crouches laughing under racing clouds. And when the sky waters her, she is running through an air-flung sea: hair flying and slapping, she is wet and wet. Storm screaming above her, across her, through her (as he had). Battered, torn by the fury of air and water, she is exhilarated. She is life. From her animal throat, she joins her howl to the wind and they join and part, join and part, as hot as thunder. They are the storm, and she is filled, until, screaming out, she falls and claws her way into the earth to rest.

Time cannot be linear, else why does his scent on your fingers last only an instant while separation is an eternity? Neither is it elastic – elastic only stretches and returns, it cannot shrink, and time expands and contracts as the breast of a sleeping beauty rises and falls. Time is a butterfly wing, a curl of smoke, a head cold, a sunset, a stubbed toe, a mountain, a missed train, as long as life, as brief as death. Measure my time by my heartbeat, by hair growing and falling, by the changing colours of my skin: collect my tears in your hands and count them; fold my laughter into paper planes and throw them out into the world. Here is my warm time; here is my still time; here is my blood time. Whole continents will be born and die with each breath I take; a mouse will blink once in my lifetime. I am inside and outside time. Time moves around and through me. I make time. We flow.

'Time flows. Let me go back to our time.'

Small and green, the apples. She is watching them, touching their outline with her fingers lightly against the blurred glass. Not seeing, she is frozen, still. There is no face in the trees. Her life is as long as it takes her to smoke a cigarette, to drink tea, to finish a crossword. And then the rest will follow. All of their time moves through her head, one time at a time: there has been no time since he left. She kisses each one lightly. They are cruel, and she grazes her mouth against them and tastes iron. But she holds them to her. She fills the empty place where he was with thoughts of her own cold death.

Homecoming

Do not die. You are the brown girl, and there are other faces. Come now. Awake.

'I choose now.'

At the end of her recipe, she sighs and finds herself in her own place. She lights a cigarette, walks into the end of her day, and looks around at her life. Clearing the old mess from her room and her heart, she finds a photograph of herself sunbathing in the garden. She smiles and peers out of her window. After a moment, leaving the linear world at the door, she sheds her mundane skin and pads out into the garden, where a face waits for her in the leaves.

Jon Nash

WALKING WITH ORION

I walk the winter
in lockstep with Orion.
Bright Betelgeuse and Bellatrix
stars at my shoulders.

In the dying days
of summer I search for him,
flaming fist gripping a club,
rising in the east.

As he chases
seven pleiadean sisters
across the sky again and again,
we rise together.

Over a thousand years
ago the light of his sword
left the heart of a nebula
to meet me tonight.

I watch three canoes
glide over ink black waters
their star story just beginning
Already ending.

Dog star by his side,
and taking me by the hand,
he teaches me the winter songs
'til April returns.

Ancient and modern,
we travel in time spirals,
arms outstretched and standing strong
'til I fall out of step.

STAR TIME

Some of the stars that our ancestors spoke with
died out oh so long ago.
Their life giving light now travelling through
space as memory gives way to entropy.

They still burn, still speak, still turn our heads upward,
craning our ears to listen.
'Oh listen child we are so much older
our counsel died long before you were born'.

Some nights I look up and feel small and holy,
just as my ancestors did,
the closest I will get to time travel,
past painted on the sky for me to see.

And far stars act as our cosmic memory.
Stories of deep time.
We circle the sun and repeat and repeat,
our bodies growing, ageing by the light.

Homecoming

The rich iron in our blood was forged in a star
as it collapsed and fell.
A moment of creation, never past
but ever present and unfolding still.

Nancy M Bell

MYTHS AND DREAMS

My name is Maighri. I speak to you of a time when the earth was young and still shining from Creation. This is my story, and in a way, it is yours as well.

Once I knew a man, not an ordinary man. How I met him, or when I knew him, is of no consequence and would reveal secrets in the telling that are not entirely mine to tell. Let it suffice to say he was as young as tomorrow and as old as time. He was not a tall man, yet when you looked at him he filled your vision. Black his hair was, and thick like a mane about his shoulders, his brown eyes always filled with mischief. He was my mate, my husband, although ours were no normal vows taken in a Christian house. Rather, they were ceremonies reaching back into the misty recesses of legend.

We were joined, near as I can recall, on a beautiful green hill in Eire. Close to the mystic places on ancient holy ground. We were attended by our guests, both seen and unseen. In the passage of time I have forgotten the true significance of our union. We pledged ourselves by the earth, wind, water, and fire. I stood beside him in the hollow of the green hill, our faces to the west. Our eyes met and a power and a great light came upon us. We were soaring high above in the blue sky oblivious to anything except each other and the wind in our wings.

When at last we settled back to the hill the wind in my feathers became once again the rustle of my skirts. Turing to the east, we joined our souls and the shift came upon us once more. We raced across the valley, heads tossing and manes swept back with the wind of our passing. Drinking the wind like water we flew across the earth our manes entwined so close did we move together. Three circuits we made before halting with loud snorts and touches of our soft muzzles. The world shimmered and when it cleared we were curled in the base of a massive hollow tree. The floor covered in soft wood chips and the sun streaming in through splits high in the trunk. We were safe and cared for as a child in the womb cradled in the heart of the oak. We slept and dreamed dreams of incredible beauty though neither of us could ever remember exactly what it was we dreamed. I awoke to the voice of fire, no ordinary fire this, it shone and crackled and sparked all about us, but did not burn. The flames leaped high above us; our guest told us later you could see the conflagration to the coast of the sea. When we came to ourselves again we were alone on the high green hill, the wedding guests gone leaving us to our own reverie, content we were well and truly married. A misting of rain blessed us with its touch.

Sligo, for that was his name, opened his brown eyes and smiled at me in the early dawn light. We dressed slowly and went arm in arm down the hill to feed our horses. He had a way with animals, my man, and especially horses. I think perhaps he was a pooka, but my memory fails me on that point. However, between us we could charm the best from any horse or pony. We saved some from the knackers and rescued others from cruel owners. What sad stories they told us, hard work with no food and no thanks for staying when they could have fared better in the hills. They rewarded us with loyalty and friendship; we were never without friends in times of need in the hills.

He was a good man, my Sligo, never able to stand cruelty or injustice. We were happy, though the land suffered under a blight. Humans and animals; oldsters and babes alike starved and died; Death's hand indiscriminately took them both. It tore my heart to hear their little souls crying and pleading for the life they would never know.

Homecoming

Finally, I too became great with child, and on the cold eve of Imbolc I lay down on the green turf to bring forth life and fertility. It was not an easy birth and before it was half done I knew I would trade my life for my son's. Sligo saw the truth of it as well, he held me and wept, his tears falling to mix with the dew in the moonlight. Our animals and the ponies from the hills stood about me in a ring, silent in the silver moonshine. My own mare stood by my head, her muzzle soft on my cheek, breathing life into my body until I could find the strength to bring life into this world. Across the heavens I heard the wailing of the dying and held fast to the rhythm of the mare's breathing. The dogs curled close for warmth and the ponies whuffled in sympathy.

At last he came from my body into a glorious dawn, a strong man child, born at that moment between night and morning with the sun in the eastern sky and the moon lingering in the west. I could not give him all my power, some things must be withheld from a man child, but I freely gave what I could. I hope it will be enough.

Then I left them, my Sligo and my son, with the mare's promise to feed him. The keening in the heavens ceased, fertility seeping back into the land as my blood soaked through the grass into the brown earth of the hill.

This myth comes to you from the beginning of time. It was the end of one age and the dawning of a new one. As always, there was sorrow as well as joy.

Homecoming

Liz Cruse

INFINITE MATRYOSHI

Times within Times – The Infinite Russian Dolls

In the October of 2023, as Time is defined by Homo sapiens of the post-Enlightenment world, a common garden spider hitched a ride on the wing mirror of my car. She wove a web over the mirror and took shelter between the glass and its casing. I thought she would blow away but in her shelter on the planet of my car she survived.

One day I opened the car to find my stowaway in the door cavity. Let me bring her inside I thought, out of the wild terrestrial winds induced by driving. But she scuttled away. I thought her lost until drifts of gossamer began to appear down near the passenger seat.

I had hopes for her survival. I carry bags of cuttings to the dump so dead leaves and various small creatures find their way into the car. The occasional snail crawls up onto the interior roof, slugs attach themselves to the carpet in the boot and small flies rise from the branches, hoping in their tiny fly minds to get out into the wider air. Surely she would trap some of these small creatures to eat.

Through the winter I forgot about her but then in January of this year, I pulled my sunshade down to block the low winter rays. In the left-hand corner behind the shield was a small creamy egg sac, densely woven and clinging to it, dead, the sole spider inhabitant of my car.

Some spider eggs overwinter and hatch in spring. I have left this touching evidence of the will to survive where it is and live in hope. I am beginning to suspect that hope is empty. (After I had written this piece, on 13th

April, I found my windscreen dotted with spiderlings some of which I was able to liberate to the air outside.)

Most UK spiders live for a year, some three. My passenger's life was probably cut short due to insufficient food, assuming she hatched in the previous spring. Her lifespan probably only extended for three quarters of its natural length. In human terms perhaps some sixty years of a projected lifespan of eighty years.

Did she have any sense of being cut off from the world where she began her life somewhere in the flowers and bushes of my garden? Or did my car just seem to be her world. If her offspring hatch how will they survive? Perhaps there are still small flies in the car. Inside my house I find webs and areas where the desiccated carcasses of fruit flies adhere miserably to the architrave of a window: a spider's larder. Tiny insects whose lives are contained within the time of the spider.

The spider's existence from October 2023 to January 2023 coincided with four months of my life that began 70 years ago when I was born onto planet Earth, summoned out of my mother by the time that had elapsed since my conception, tied here by gravity but able, like the spider, to move. On maturity I could find new places to live with the illusion at least of free will. But as the spider is blown by the currents of the air so am I caught in the tides of social and historical circumstance, with less free will than I imagine.

The Time that dragged me through the iron gates of life was a hopeful one. She took me in her arms and carried me towards the slow and from my perspective now, golden, times of childhood. Time was a leisurely choreographing games of fantasy that were lifetimes. Time brushed her fingers over flowers and sharp-edged leaves drawing my attention so that I sat sometimes for days (though only an hour maybe, maybe only five minutes) in front of an aster bearing a bumble bee.

Time has conducted me through cities in three continents: London, Swansea, Hong Kong, Delhi, New

York, Seattle, Florence, Bristol where I have made homes of varying duration.

Time has led me into occupations and wound my life up with other species, both human and animal, sometimes in long multiply stranded threads, sometimes in webs and sometimes leaving my existence as a single strand that drifts until it finds some new place to attach itself.

Now, I have less time left than I have already lived. I feel the impulse towards meeting with Time as I did in my childhood – unquestioningly absorbed so that each moment stretches out like an infinity of spider thread, breaking only to reveal another translucent filament forming.

Yet mostly I flick through the minutes, hours and days as if through a blank diary that I must fill with words and impressions. Time's leaves must not be wasted. They must be anticipated, planned, completed as richly as possible. Yet how easy it is to be scarcely aware that one or two or three have been turned over at once, unmarked.

For the moment, Time consorts with me in Glastonbury. There is a lane at the bottom of the Tor, a holloway as it starts out, where there is a narrow seam of clay. The stones revealed as the earth crumbles away often turn out to be fragments of ammonites.

In the first quarter of the 21st Century I hold in my hand a fragment of a creature homo sapiens has classed as a cephalopod, probably most closely related to modern squid and cuttlefish, more distantly to the nautilus. It could have been alive 200 million years ago, perhaps less. The animals died out 66 million years ago probably due to the same meteoric disaster that ended the existence of dinosaurs. The fossil, though broken, will nevertheless survive me for thousands, even millions of years more until crushed or eroded to powder, or dissolved gradually in acid rain.

In the 17th century Athanasius Kircher wondered if fossils were produced by petrifying 'juices' that flowed underground hardening animals into stone but also conjuring images to enchant and educate. Time as a magician. Time as alchemist.

The ammonite swam in the warm Jurassic seas for perhaps 4 – 36 years then petrified in rock roughly 200million years ago.. Its stone facsimile shifted with the slow movements of the earth's crust until it emerged in a lane in Somerset. Its time, living and dead, encompasses mine so vastly that compared to it I am only a scintillation of consciousness. Even my bones will not outlast it.

But the time of Earth vastly contains that of the ammonite. Some 4.4 billion years ago (4000 million years) Earth coalesced into something that, had humans been able to see it, would have been recognisable as a world and perhaps, even then supportive of extremophile life that went beyond rock and gas. It had stable continents and liquid water, a temperature probably less than 100 degrees Centigrade. But molten lava still formed great areas of the planet and there was no oxygen.

Earth has been in existence over a thousand times longer than the ammonite in its animal and rock forms. The planet is likely to live beyond the many armed cephalopod for another 2 billion years from now. At this point we humans will be long gone as Sun's light intensifies, and evaporates the oceans with searing luminescence. But Time will play with the Sun for another 5 billion years or so after that. Helios will grow to Red Giant, shrink to White Dwarf. At long last it will die, the billions of years of its heat consumed by Time. Sol will lose the bright and coloured clothing that marks it as a main sequence star. It will slip into invisibility though something of it will remain just as the stone trace remains of the ammonite.

Our Sun pre-dates Earth and will outlive it. Sol, the centre of our Solar System, will become an ultra-cool dwarf star in the end. This is the state of a weakly shining star in the constellation of Aquarius that human scientists have called Trappist 1.

Trappist 1 allowed itself to be seen at the end of our 20th Century in 1999. At the beginning of our human-defined 3rd Millennium, it was announced to humanity. It was in existence at least a billion or two years before the birth of our Solar System. This pale star is expected to shine on for ten trillion years. This is 700 times longer than the present age of the Universe. But Time is beyond the restrictions of exactitude at these vast reaches of years.

Trappist 1 will see the end of our Sun and all its attendant planets.

Trappist 1 is orbited by 7 planets. The light that reaches them is dim. Their skies would never be brighter than Earth's sky at sunset; only a little brighter than a night of a full moon. Three of them may be capable of sustaining life. We humans will for the foreseeable far future only know this by remote analysis since Trappist 1 is over 40 light years away from Earth. Using our fastest spacecraft as of now it would take 2,958 years to travel one light year. The Universe presents us with its mathematics and laughs at our pretensions.

The Time of the Universe encapsulates Our Sun, Trappist 1 and all the beings of Outer and Inner Space. The Universe began – maybe – 13.8 billion years ago. Is there a Time still greater that encloses the lifespan of the Universe itself? Or does the Time which we try to grasp and confine with our poetic and mathematical perceptions become no more than a wraith at Universal and quantum levels?

Perhaps there are those who can answer with equations. I will rest with Time as companion, psychopomp, alchemist, magician. She of infinite guises who always holds within her manifestations the times of other beings, on and on, beyond my gaze.

This piece is dedicated to my friend Alexander Alexandrovich Krotov, mathematician and computer whizz who was never truly at home on Earth. His lifespan 1974 – 2021 will be enclosed within mine when my life, that began in 1953, ends. So are dolls enclosed inside each other in the matryoshki of his native Russia.

Viv Rimmer

BONES

Soft white bones in the soil
Generous, crumbling into the earth
Like ash, forever cycling.
Whose are they?

A drizzle starts to fall. A light comes on
In a distant house.
I dig my fingers deep around them.
Whose are they?
Better they stay dead.

Pinpoint stars above suck the brains out of my head
Up into the abyss.
The world turns upside down.
I hang onto the earth, good mother,
Through my hungry grasping feet.
Who am I?

Aine King

SCHOOL TIME

Hurry UP!
Mam's voice leaping up the stairs as I leap down them
and don't –
JUMP from the third step -
BANG
the floorboard holds another day.
Over my shoulder the fourth step teases
Not yet but soon.
Crammed with cornflakes, racing the toaster.
Floor-footed, anchored feet unswinging.
A sun-shard slips across the table square by square.
The buckle-tooth gnaws the bag-strap
and the shoe-strap
hole by hole to the end of their tethers.
Mam's quick kiss is unreached for.
Not yet but soon
I'll leave my coat at home to shrink and shorten.
All winter the door latch has been dropping to my reach.
Daffodils dance knee-high and bee-full.
I am giant and unfearful of
the tide
playing hide-and-seek with the bones
of our grandfather's father's boat
built when the shingle was stones.
Redshank, Turnstone, Dipper, Dipper, Grebe
I am full of birds
wide as a cormorant

racing the long pale heron upwards over the hill
to school.
Hurry UP
Not yet but soon
the bell will hammer us in
for morning prayers
and Purgatory,
sums
beyond my short reach
for ever and ever
on the tear-cockled ink-bled Small Squares of BIG Class
and Sister Michael Mary, ticking like a clock.

Liudmila Nikanorova

RELIGION AND CALENDARS: SAKHA MOONS AND SUMMER SOLSTICE

For centuries, even for millennia, human life and activities have been measured in time. While the majority of people are now used to the standardised units of time, such as seconds, minutes, hours, days, months, and years, the organisation of these units through calendars can be very diverse. There are over forty calendars in use today. Some of them are sun-based, like the Gregorian solar calendar used in the UK since 1750. There are also lunisolar calendars that follow the movements of the moon, like the Chinese, Jewish, and Islamic calendars. Religion is closely intertwined with the organisation of calendars. Holidays in different countries can indicate which religion has the strongest presence in the nation-state. In most European countries, for example, Christmas and Easter are the largest public holidays indicating the strong presence of Christianity in Europe. Another example is when the Soviet Union introduced new holidays to replace the Orthodox Christian ones following the Russian Revolution in 1917. This measure was supposed to mark the transition from the "dark religious" Russian Empire to the "modern secular" Soviet state, where religion was regarded as "the opium of the people."

The names of the units of time can also inform about the main activities of the people. The calendar of the Sakha (Yakut) people from North-East Asia, for instance, reflects environmental and agricultural cycles central to the life of the Sakha. This is particularly evident in the Sakha names of months:

Kulun Tutar yia [March] – the month of foal catching.

Sakha people have been historically horse herders and have incorporated products made from mare's milk into their diet. During this month, foals are captured and separated from the mares to facilitate the milking process. Kymys, a drink made from fermented mare's milk, is not only a local delicacy but an important part of Sakha ceremonies and festivities.

Muus ustar yia [April] – the month of ice drift.

Sakha Sire [Sa. 'the land of the Sakha'] is located in one of the coldest regions of the planet, where rivers and lakes freeze during the winter months. The thawing of the Lena River, one of the largest rivers in the world, is a time of excitement but also anxiety, as it often leads to the annual floods in the region.

Yem yia [May] – the month of spawning.

Lake fishing, especially for sobo, a fish belonging to the same family as carp, has been one of the main subsistence practices among the Sakha. This month marks the spawning season for sobo fish.

Bes yia [June] – the month of a pine tree.

This month not only indicates the arrival of summer, when trees turn green, but also the specific period for harvesting resin from the Siberian pine.

Ot yia [July] – the month of hay.

Although the Sakha strongly identify with horse-herding, their primary economy has been revolving around cattle-herding for centuries. Given that winters can last up to nine months, cattle require significant quantities of pre-prepared hay. Thus, haymaking is one of the most important activities for many Sakha households.

Atyrd'akh yia [August] – the month of hay-stacking.

This month indicates the stage of hay-stacking, which takes place after the hay has been dried in the sun for several days, sometimes weeks.

Balağan yia [September] – the month of balağan.

Balağan is a Sakha wooden dwelling, in which most Sakha lived until the early 20th century. During the summer months, the Sakha lived in summer dwellings called saiylyk, and in the winter months in balağan. The construction of balağan effectively maintained warmth even in temperatures dropping below -60 °C. This month marks the end of summer and move to the winter dwelling balagan.

As you may have understood by now, the word yia, or yi, means 'month' in Sakha. It also means 'moon,' which indicates how the Sakha calendar follows the movements of the moon to measure the time.

*

The largest calendar holiday of the Sakha, recorded since the 17th century, is the Yhyakh. Although it is the celebration of the summer solstice, it can be celebrated between the end of May and early July. Similar to the names of the months, Yhyakh is closely linked to Sakha practices. The term Yhyakh originates from the word 'ys,' which refers to the practice of libating kymys drink. Scholars have categorised this celebration as a religious ritual and shamanic rite for centuries. Among the contemporary Sakha, however, Yhyakh is largely described as the New Year celebration and "a day when Sakha feel Sakha."

Yhyakh has officially been recognised as a public holiday in the Sakha Republic in 1991. Before that, it was discouraged from celebration due to its religious connotations, which conflicted with Soviet anti-religious campaigns.

John Durham Peters (2012) argues in his research that calendars are never neutral maps, and are devices of the political and religious organisation. Yhyakh, the Sakha celebration of the summer solstice, is just one of many examples that demonstrate how calendar celebrations can be used to situate and historicise important political and societal events.

Jennifer Uzzell

CONVERSATIONS WITH THE CAILLEACH

Winter 20/21

Old Woman walks the land.
Looks on the fields, the cities, the smoke, the noise,
The constant dizzying light.

Veiled One, Bone Mother.
Where are her wild places? Her solitude?
Where are the herds? The aurochs? The bears?
The cranes? The wolves? The mammoths?
She remembers, and she mourns.
In the middle distance she sees a small fire
Burning on the darkening hillside.
Sighing she walks towards it.

* * * * * * * * * * * * *

I am sitting on a hillside under an apple tree,
Watching the full moon rise huge and golden.
My breath catches at the beauty of it all-
The changing blue of the twilight sky
The land set out below me like a cloak stretching
To the shining silver line of the sea in the distance.
It is getting cold. I shiver, and huddle a little closer to the fire.

Out of the darkness behind me an old woman approaches.
She sits beside me for a while in companionable silence.
We both stare into the flames and I wonder

what she sees there.
After a while, still with no words,
she takes off her green mantle
And places it around my shoulders.
In my mind I can hear the voice of my Nan speaking.
"It's cold out there…don't forget your scarf!"
Is it still there, I wonder?

* * * * * * * * * * * * *

A cottage by the path where no cottage ever was.
Where no cottage should be.
Ancient. Turf-roofed.
Smoke drifts up from the eaves
into the sharp morning air.
The door creaks slowly open.

Inside, the smell of wood-smoke
A cheerful fire blazes bright against the dark room.
By it, a large black cat raises her head, regards me with disinterest, and goes back to sleep.
At the table, an old woman smiles-gestures towards a chair and I sit
"Who are you?" I ask. "What is this place?
It didn't used to be here."
She frowns impatiently.
"Wrong questions!" she snaps.
"Why am I here?"
She smiles now. "Better.
There are some interesting things on the cards
for you. See?"
And she pushes a deck of cards towards me spread out face down.
I choose one and turn it over - "The Long Road".

On it an old woman - perhaps this old woman -
it's hard to tell,

Homecoming

is walking away from me leaning on a staff. She is
walking through a verdant summer wood, but in front of
her the trees are turning to the blazing colours of Autumn.
And then there is snow on the ground, and bare branches,
and the long hard cold of winter.
Still she walks on.

Suddenly it's all too much for me. All of it.
Everything that is past and lost to me forever. All that I
have to do; to be.
Everything that I have to accomplish in my tiny lifespan.
All the burdens laid upon me:
To teach; to birth not children
but words-wisdom into the world;
To comfort the bereaved and to serve the Dead, and to
bear witness to both.

Too much.
Too much.
Too much!

I slump, exhausted and fighting back panic and tears.
She looks into my face and her eyes are oceans of grief
and compassion.
"Its hard, isn't it?' she says. "Have a cup of tea!"
She smiles then, and it's as if the sun has come out from
behind the clouds.
She pours the golden steaming liquid into the teacup
And it seems to me that every welcoming hearth,
every kind word,
Every mother's hug is contained in that cup.
I sip it and feel the warmth seep through me
Bringing strength and hope and resolve.
"Grandmother," I say, "Are you a Goddess?"
She laughs then, and her eyes sparkle with mischief
"Goodness me, no, dear!" she says,
"I'm much older
than that!"

Homecoming

* * * * * * * * * * * * *

A cave.
It's dark.
I am lying on a straw mattress on the ground
Snuggled under blankets and furs.
In the doorway a large bear is sleeping.
She stirs in her sleep from time to time, making reassuring snuffling sounds.
She will keep me safe.

In the corner, the Old Woman sits.
behind her, propped against the wall is her broom.
She notices me looking and grins. "Everything needs a clean sweep from time to time," she says, "out with the old; in with the new."
And I understand. With her broom she sweeps away the centuries;
All that is finished and done with.
She is knitting. She knits the land and its stories.
She knits the future as she knitted the past.
She knits my thoughts, and my hopes and my dreams;
And possibly a scarf. "It's cold outside, after all."

I find myself thinking of all those who have been here before me.
All who have come and gone and lived and died on this land.
Leaving no trace. No memory. No echo.

In the corner she stirs,
Old Woman, Bone Mother, Veiled One.
The black cat peers out at me from between her apron folds and blinks sleepily.
She remains unimpressed - if she remembers me at all.
"It's all ok, you know," the old woman offers. "They're all here."
"Who are?" I ask, looking around me.

Homecoming

"All of them. Your long mothers and long fathers. All of
them.
Right back to the very first people who walked on these
islands.
I remember them all; their hopes, their fears, their tears
and their laughter.
They're all here," she says. "In my Dreaming."
She taps her head, Old Woman, Veiled One,
Bone Mother.
"And what is remembered lives."

Jack Wolf

AFTERWORD / FLYSTRIKE

Before the invention and imposition of capitalist-industrialist notions of Time, which did not happen fully until our modern era, it was not uncommon for Western people to experience its passage very differently from the ways in we, as modern people, tend to do – as an experience that is structured predominantly by a forward linear travel from one point to another, the progress of which may be measured by some sort of clock. We do not, however, have to go back very far to find a cultural experience that is either somewhat, or radically, different. For example, in Britain prior to the establishment of the railways, it was unnecessary for Time measured even in this way to be standardised across the whole nation – Greenwich meantime did not, for instance, cover the whole of the British Isles until 1847 as noon was still determined by the highest point of the sun in any locality rather by than bureaucratic convenience, falling up to 15 minutes later in the west of the country than in London. Time was, of course, still parcelled out into the familiar system of regular minutes, hours, days, weeks, and so on – the concept of measurable and standardisable time was already embedded in Western thought and society.

But going further back, let's say to the 14th century, a time long before a mechanical clock became a common feature in people's homes, we find an era in which daily time was measured in natural stretches whose duration was subject to change depending on the time of year and latitude of the observer – meaning afternoon would naturally be longer in Summer than in Winter, and a Winter night up to three times longer than its Midsummer equivalent. Daytime was not separable from daylight, or evening from the approach of dusk. The rhythms of the years were set primarily by the rhythms of the agricultural seasons as well as those of the sun and moon, and for most people, most of the time, this was enough. Only the needs of the Church required greater accuracy – sundials indicating hours and hourly fractions were commonplace in religious settings – although the religious calendar was not fully disconnected from the rhythms and flows of natural time, tethering the date of Easter to both the moon and the Spring Equinox. For most people, the passage and lived human experience of Time was not separable from the rhythms of the natural world and was inevitably subordinated to them – there was no turning on the electric lights and central heating to pretend nights and winters away for your average mediaeval peasant, monk, or friar.

We don't need to leave the UK to go back considerably further than this and into a rather different system of reckoning – the era of the Stone Circle builders. The calendar theory of Stonehenge, which is situated on Salisbury Plain in Wiltshire, suggests that in addition to its focus on the well known Winter Solsticial alignment, this most famous of Stone Circles represents the passage of a solar year divided mathematically into months, potentially to allow a religious elite to calculate the exact times and dates for certain rituals, just as the 14th century church required the same precision in its calculation of Saints' Days. If the calendar theory is correct, then the liturgical year of this early Bronze Age culture was even more deeply embedded in the passage of circular Time as governed by natural forces than the later Christian Church, despite any ritual pressures that may have also acted on it. For the builders of Stonehenge, the calendar year seems to have been, both for peasantry and religious elite, fully embedded in the real world of farming, weather, and the cycles of the sun. How they conceptualised the passage of Time we cannot know – but it may have been conceived as an ongoing series of cycles rather than a single forward motion, giving rise, perhaps, to ideas of reincarnation similar to those found in certain present day Indigenous kinship systems who hold that Human Spirits are reborn every three generations.

Thus far, all these ideas have suggested to us reckoning systems of one sort or another, which in turn implies that, for Humans at least, our experience of Time is inseparable from our ability to measure it. But this is not inevitably the case: many meditative practises seek to focus on the moment and release us from the onward march of linear time. Neither is it the case that, where such systems exist, they were, or even are, invariably linear and forward facing. Just as the Stonehenge calendar works within a repeating cycle, the modern Pagan concept of the wheel of the year introduces – or reintroduces – the idea of Time as an ever-recurring circularity.

Can we go further back and find potential systems of thought that may perhaps do away with the idea of regular reckoning altogether? In theory and in imagination, we can, though the theory becomes shakier and the imagination correspondingly wilder. In 2023, Paul Pettitt of Durham University and independent researcher Ben Bacon proposed the idea that certain symbols in Paleolithic cave art represent a reckoning system of sorts, based on the mating and birthing times of various species. This would be a calendar of a type entirely unknown to us, whose starting point would be located not in the solar or lunar years but in something else entirely – the seasonal melting of river ice. Allowing for a little variability in the exact timing of this event produces a year whose beginning may fall on a slightly different date in each cycle, meaning these may be of differing lengths – a year with a particularly long and hard winter may perhaps have been counted as a long year and one with an early melt a short one – or the other way round. And following this idea, perhaps the year ended with the onset of Winter, and the long cold time was not counted within normal Time at all: perhaps it was something else, something sacred, or terrible. Perhaps Winter belonged to the dead. Equally, perhaps, given the difficulty of undertaking lengthy hunting trips in temperatures well below zero, it may have been a time for re-establishing social bonds among the living: a set aside Time defined not by the weather or the calendar, but by family relationships. This, then, would be a notion of Time as a matrix whose very nature changes, or is changed, depending on what is going on in the everyday, earthbound world, as opposed to being dictated or measured by something in the heavens; a world where Time itself is somehow generated out of natural events of which humans are a part.

In his seminal 1997 book *The Spell of the Sensuous*, David Abrams argues that certain societies situate the future and the past in physical Place – over the horizon and below the ground respectively. He goes on to suggest that in an oral culture, narrative, time, and place are inseparable in profound ways that end up building up a story in a very different way from that encountered within a culture whose understanding of all these things is recorded, if not actively filtered, through the technology of writing. It might not be too much of a stretch to infer from this that an oral understanding of Time itself can be partly constructed out of the ways in which Time is included in story – a very different approach from the modernist one with which we are so familiar, as story and reality connect in a mutual dependency, out of which human knowledge is created. Such a way of thinking implies that we create our Time as much as we experience it. Creation and Human understanding of the thing created give rise to a temporal reality in which people are fully active participants. Put more simply, if Time needs to be storied in order to exist, it needs Storytellers to give it meaning.

This speculation may be not entirely dissimilar to a construction of Time embedded in the Aboriginal concept of The Dreaming. The Dreaming, however, is not 'a time' in the sense of it having a fixed temporal locality – it is not in the past, nor in the future, nor is it simply in the present as human beings experience it – and it is instructive that none of the Aboriginal languages has a word for 'Time' in the English sense. It is perhaps better to think of The Dreaming as a series of ongoing relationships that stretch across and through both time and land, binding together the worlds of spirit and flesh and regulating conduct across them, operating both everywhere and everywhen. On the other hand, Aboriginal mythologies do include a number of Creation myths which touch upon events taking place within the Dreaming that may be happening in the past. Ancestral Spirits walk across the bare land leaving flora and fauna in their tracks; relationships between things are established, connections forged; Spirits transform into landscape features, wherein they remain. The ongoing presence of the Spirits in the landscape keeps them close by and means that Creation continues indefinitely. This idea of ongoing Creation, of course, is not a million miles away from modern theories of evolution or of the putative behaviour of quantum particles around a black hole. It is also not unlike the emergence of the ten Sephirot from the Ain Soph in the Jewish Qabala. But it is a very long way from clock-based, forward moving notions of linear Time.

The various pieces in this issue deal with ways of viewing Time differently from the modern norm. Sometimes they seem not to deal with Time at all, but with Place: in 'Unexploded Ordnance and Toxic Waste', Harriet Sams talks about her visit to an ex-military site in Cumbria and witnessing the ongoing consequences of long forgotten Human decisions. Heidi Smith's poem 'The Orkney Islands', and Nimue Brown's short essay 'Tide and Time Wait Forever', explore relationships between human bodies and landscapes over geological time, while Hannah Semple's poem 'Earth Time' suggests how the flow of Time may mirror the movement of sand trapped on a beach. In a similar vein, in 'Walking with Orion', Jon Nash considers the long view of Time as it connects Human lives with those of Stars. Other pieces wrestle with the experience of Time from varying Human and Non-Human perspectives – Liz Cruse, in 'Infinite Matryoshi', explores the conception of lifetimes within lifetimes, while Aine King's poem 'School Time' deals with a child's experience of time passing, which is very different from an adult's. Other pieces, such as Sharon Shaw's 'The Stag Bar', Jennifer Uzzell's 'Conversations with the Cailleach', and Nancy M. Bell's 'Myths and Dreams' explore the notion of myth-making, and imagine different histories within imaginary and mythic worlds not so far away from our own, where time works differently. Morgain Merch Lleued, in her short story 'Time Dance', asks whether Time exists inside or outside of us, and Gordon Maclellan's poems 'Black Poplar' and 'Vigil' challenge us to consider the connections between ancient past and present, and to experience time as other beings may do. Finally the collection begins and ends with academic contributions from Ronald Hutton and Liudmilla Nikanorova, who respectively explore the relationships between ancient and contemporary traditional peoples and the Sun and Moon.

FLYSTRIKE

Today I'll go
to the cold upland beyond Sibleyback
to the open land where feral ponies
congregate and sheep wear their tails long.
No risk of fly-strike here. Today, no fear
of fog. The rain-white stones
sparkle in the grey fuzz of the dawn

where thirty thousand years ago, the wind
(here, where the land is highest, here
where sky is heavy as a press)
carved cheesewrings out of granite
and wrung the water from the stark
fruit land, the stacked circles of stone,

bearing nuggets of bright casserite, white tin.
Now all the seams are all worked out, the copper engine
house Wheal Phoenix derelict. Tourists swarm in the
hotel, the Hurlers halt. Welcome to Minions.
Caradon Hill transmitter buzzes
on the other side of the grey moor:
Television signals; fog-lamps; fly-struck red.

List of Contributors

Ronald Hutton is Professor of History at the University of Bristol. His research specialises in early modern Britain, British folklore, pre-Christian religion, and modern paganism. He can currently be found online lecturing at Gresham College, where he has been Professor of Divinity since 2022. His many publications include *The Triumph of the Moon: A History of Modern Pagan Witchcraft* (Oxford University Press, 1999) and *Blood and Mistletoe: a History of the Druids in Britain* (Yale University Press, 2009). His most recent work is *Queens of the Wild: Pagan Goddesses in Christian Europe: An Investigation* (Yale, 2022)

Hannah Semple is a long time Pagan and poet based in South Wales, where nature has always been her teacher and inspiration. Her poetry and nature writing can be found at **earthmothernaturelover.wordpress.com**

Heidi Hanley finds inspiration in the beautiful landscapes of New England and the wisdom of the Druid path. She hopes her poetry will inspire others to help protect and heal this beautiful, precious planet we call 'Home'. She posts some of her poetry on Facebook: **@heidihanleyauthor** and on Instagram: **@heidi_hanley**

Sharon Shaw lives in Lincolnshire with her husband Alex and their child, Willow. Sharon edits Alex's book series and audio drama, New Century, and for the last decade they have co-hosted the School of Movies podcast, enabling her to overthink Hollywood franchises and talk at delighted length about neurodiversity in film. *The Stag*

Bar has appeared in anthologies published by the author and by **Lincs and Inks.**

Gordon MacLellan is a writer, poet and storyteller whose work explores the relationships between people, places, passion and wildlife. As Creeping Toad, he works with community groups to find ways of celebrating those relationships. Other writings include *Old Stones and Ancient Bones* (poems, direct from Gordon) and *Sacred Animals* (Green Magic Books, 2023) 'Vigil' was first published in *Waiting for the Snow,* (Creeping Toad, 2024) Find out more: **creepingtoad.blogspot.com** Social media: **creeping toad**

Harriet Sams teaches, mentors, and facilitates archaeotherapy. She co-hosts online conversations with ecological creators, thinkers and writers for the charity Radical Joy for Hard Times, and co-facilitates imaginal workshops for the Climate Psychology Alliance. She writes about interconnected threads such as myth, archaeology, Earth-based spirituality, environmental art, and climate/ecological chaos. **www.nwyfre-earth.co**

Nimue Brown is an animist on the Druid path. She's a longstanding blogger at **www.druidlife.wordpress.com** and the author of assorted Pagan and Druid titles, published by Moon Books and also self-published. She lives on the Cotswold edge above the Severn River, and talks to everything.

Morgaine Merch Lleued is an Associate Lecturer in Creative Writing, a novelist and poet. Her poetry has appeared in many publications, including *The Interpreter's House*, *Orbis, The Frogmore Papers, Ink, Sweat & Tears, Antiphon, Bare Fiction* and *Iota.*

Jon Nash is a poet, playwright, theatre director and Druid based in Devon, England. His work explores truth in the digital age, our relationship with the wild during the climate crisis and animism. You can find him at **jonnash.uk** and on Instagram at **@jonnashwriter** (for writing) and **@undertheashpod** (for Druidry).

Nancy M Bell lives in Castor, Alberta. She belongs to the Writers Guild of Alberta and is on the board of the Canadian Authors Association. Publishing credits include poetry, fiction, and non-fiction. Nancy is a horsewoman and a retired equestrian coach. She enjoys fostering rescue animals and gardening. **http://www.nancymbell.ca**

Liz Cruse is a Druid and lives in Glastonbury with her cat, Sam. Her commitment to protecting the land and fostering connection with all beings underpins her practice as Storyteller, Writer and Poet. She volunteers at Plotgate Community Farm and is on the committee of Plotgate Venture Land Trust.

Viv Rimmer is a member of OBOD and lives in Reading, UK.

Aine King is a London-Irish writer, artist, and theatre-maker now living in Orkney. Her climate crisis play, Burning Bright, won the 2023 David MacLennan Award. **https://www.aineking.net/**

Jennifer Uzzell has a PhD from Durham University where she studied under the auspices of the Centre for Death and Life Studies, based in the department of Theology and Religion. Her research focuses on death rites among contemporary Druids in the UK. In addition, she is co-owner and director of a funeral home that forms part of a growing movement in the UK towards greater openness, honesty and authenticity in the way funerals are arranged and conducted.

Liudmila Nikanorova grew up in Yakutsk and studied at the Universities of Tromso and UiT, Norway. She lectures in religious studies at the Open University, where her research centres on Indigenous religious methodologies, with a focus on Shamanism as practised by the Sakha people of the Sakha republic (Yakutsk). *Sakha Moons and the Summer Solstice* was previously published on the OU Blog, March 2024.

Jack Wolf's first novel *The Tale of Raw Head and Bloody Bones* (Chatto and Windus) was published to critical acclaim in 2013. Jack set up Aurochs Underground Press in 2022 in response to the urgent need to re-evaluate human relationships to one another and the Earth itself. Jack's second novel, *Mammoth and Crow*, was published by AUP in 2022, along with a poetry collection, *Dog Walking Weather.* Visit: **aurochspress.co.uk**

Susan Greenwood has a PhD in anthropology from Goldsmith's College, where she was a lecturer on the anthropology of religion. She has taught courses on Shamanic consciousness and Altered States of Consciousness at the University of Sussex. More information can be found at **susangreenwood.org**

Wild Soda Workshop is a photographer based in the South of England. Their work centres around recognising a sense of the uncanny in the natural world.

Note

Where contributors are based in the US, Canada or other countries where US spelling and punctuation rules are commonly used, these have been retained in accordance with the localist ethos of Animist practise.

www.ingramcontent.com/pod-product-compliance
Lightning Source LLC
Chambersburg PA
CBHW071356200726
48294CB00004B/1192

* 9 7 8 1 7 3 9 6 9 7 2 5 9 *